Ghosts OF WAR

by Tammy Gagne

CAPSTONE PRESS
a capstone imprint

Bright Idea Books are published by Capstone Press
1710 Roe Crest Drive, North Mankato, Minnesota 56003
www.mycapstone.com

Library of Congress Cataloging-in-Publication Data
Names: Gagne, Tammy, author.
Title: Ghosts of war / by Tammy Gagne.
Description: North Mankato : Capstone Press, 2019. | Series: Ghosts and hauntings | Includes bibliographical references and index.
Identifiers: LCCN 2018018704 (print) | LCCN 2018020952 (ebook) | ISBN 9781543541878 (ebook) | ISBN 9781543541472 (hardcover : alk. paper)
Subjects: LCSH: Ghosts--Juvenile literature. | Haunted places--Juvenile literature. | War--Miscellanea--Juvenile literature.
Classification: LCC BF1461 (ebook) | LCC BF1461 .G2525 2019 (print) | DDC 133.1--dc23
LC record available at https://lccn.loc.gov/2018018704

Editorial Credits
Editor: Alexis Burling
Designer: Becky Daum
Production Specialist: Colleen McLaren

Photo Credits
iStockphoto, argalis, 11, JaimePharr, 12–13, JVT, cover; Shutterstock Images, Bill Dowling, 8–9, 30–31, Darya T, 26–27, Delmas Lehman, 6–7, Everett Historical, 5, 15, 16–17, 21, 25, Mendenhall Olga, 18–19, Paul Looyen, 23, 28

Design Elements: iStockphoto, Red Line Editorial, and Shutterstock Image

TABLE OF CONTENTS

CHAPTER 1

THE GHOSTS OF Gettysburg

Many people die in war. Some people say battlefields are **haunted**. A famous one is in Pennsylvania. The Battle of Gettysburg happened there in 1863. It was part of the U.S. Civil War.

More soldiers were killed or wounded in the Battle of Gettysburg than in any other Civil War battle.

Many men died during the battle. Their bodies often did not make it home. Soldiers dug big pits for the bodies. Some people say their ghosts are stuck. They say the dead should be buried in individual **graves**. Then their ghosts can move on.

Only a small number of the soldiers who died in the battle were buried at Gettysburg National Cemetery.

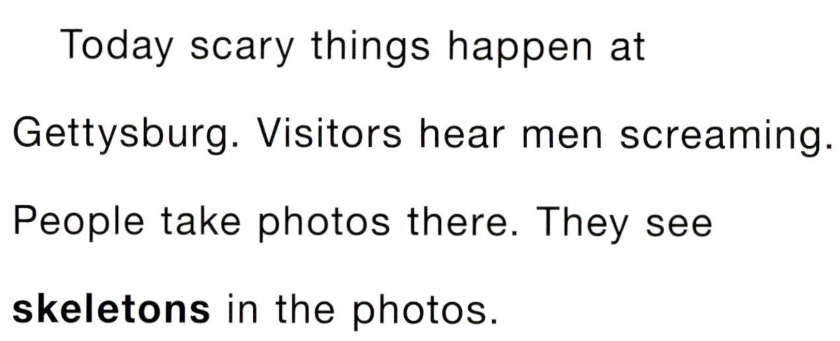

Today scary things happen at Gettysburg. Visitors hear men screaming. People take photos there. They see **skeletons** in the photos.

Some people believe Devil's Den is one of the most haunted spots on the Gettysburg battlefield.

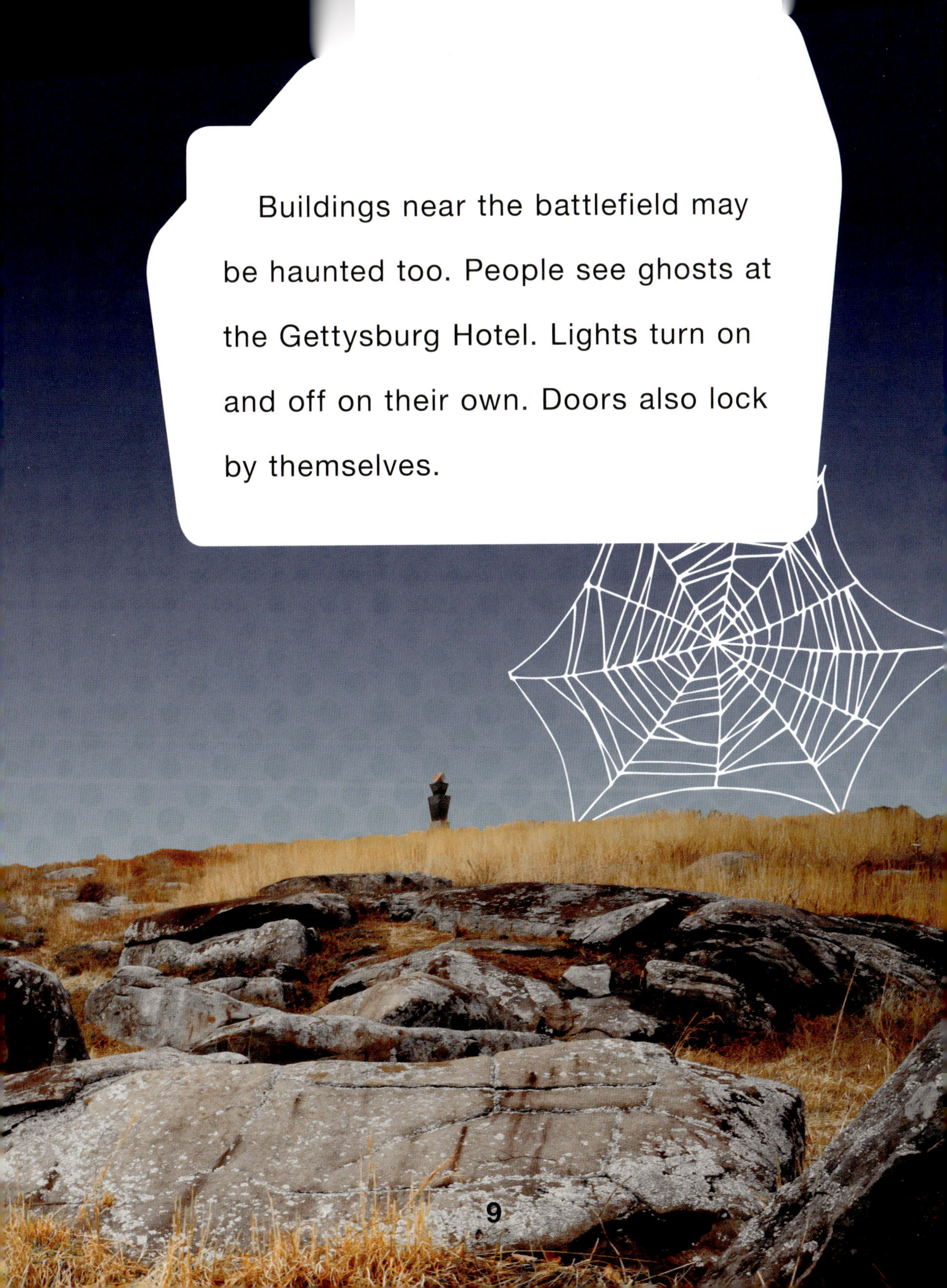

Buildings near the battlefield may be haunted too. People see ghosts at the Gettysburg Hotel. Lights turn on and off on their own. Doors also lock by themselves.

CHAPTER 2

THE GHOSTS OF Culloden

Scotland fought England in 1746. They fought at the Battle of Culloden. Scotland wanted Prince Charles Stuart to rule Great Britain. England wanted King George II. England won the battle.

Today a rock monument at the battlefield honors fallen soldiers.

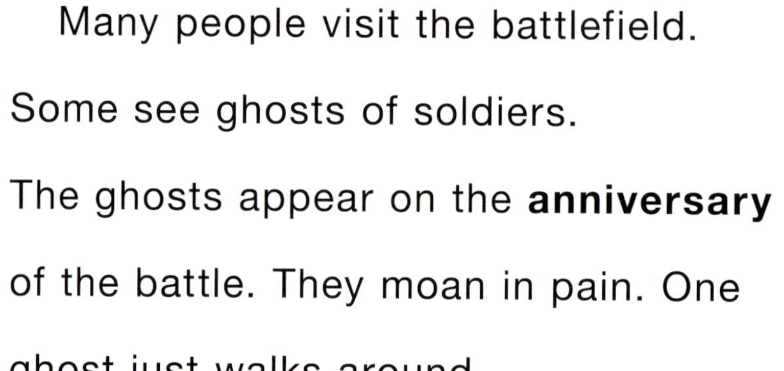

Many people visit the battlefield. Some see ghosts of soldiers. The ghosts appear on the **anniversary** of the battle. They moan in pain. One ghost just walks around.

Small headstones mark where some soldiers were buried.

SILENT GRAVES

Locals say birds do not sing near the Culloden graves. They think the birds are afraid of the ghosts.

Other ghosts seem to keep fighting. Visitors hear swords clashing. People say the ghosts do not know they are dead. They do not know the battle is over.

CHAPTER 3

THE GHOSTS OF Little Bighorn

U.S. soldiers and American Indians fought in the Battle of Little Bighorn. It was in 1876. It took place where Montana is now. The fight was bloody. Hundreds of U.S. soldiers died. Dozens of American Indians died too.

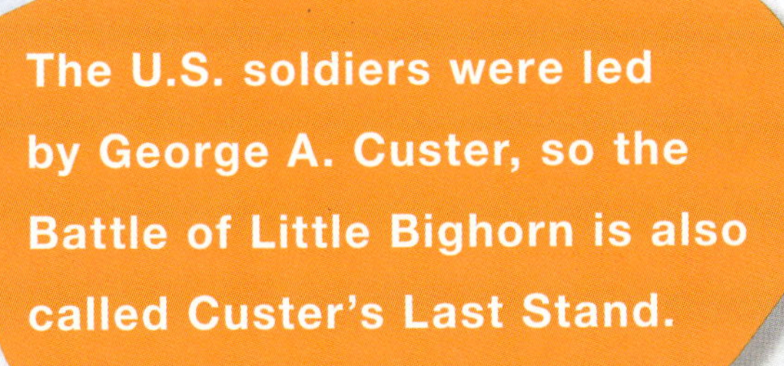

The U.S. soldiers were led by George A. Custer, so the Battle of Little Bighorn is also called Custer's Last Stand.

The U.S. Army fought two tribes. They were the Lakota Sioux and the Northern Cheyenne. The army wanted the tribes to leave the land. The tribes wanted to stay. It was their home. The tribes won the battle.

Chief Sitting Bull led the Lakota Sioux to victory at the Battle of Little Bighorn.

There is a graveyard next to the visitor center. Many U.S. soldiers are buried there.

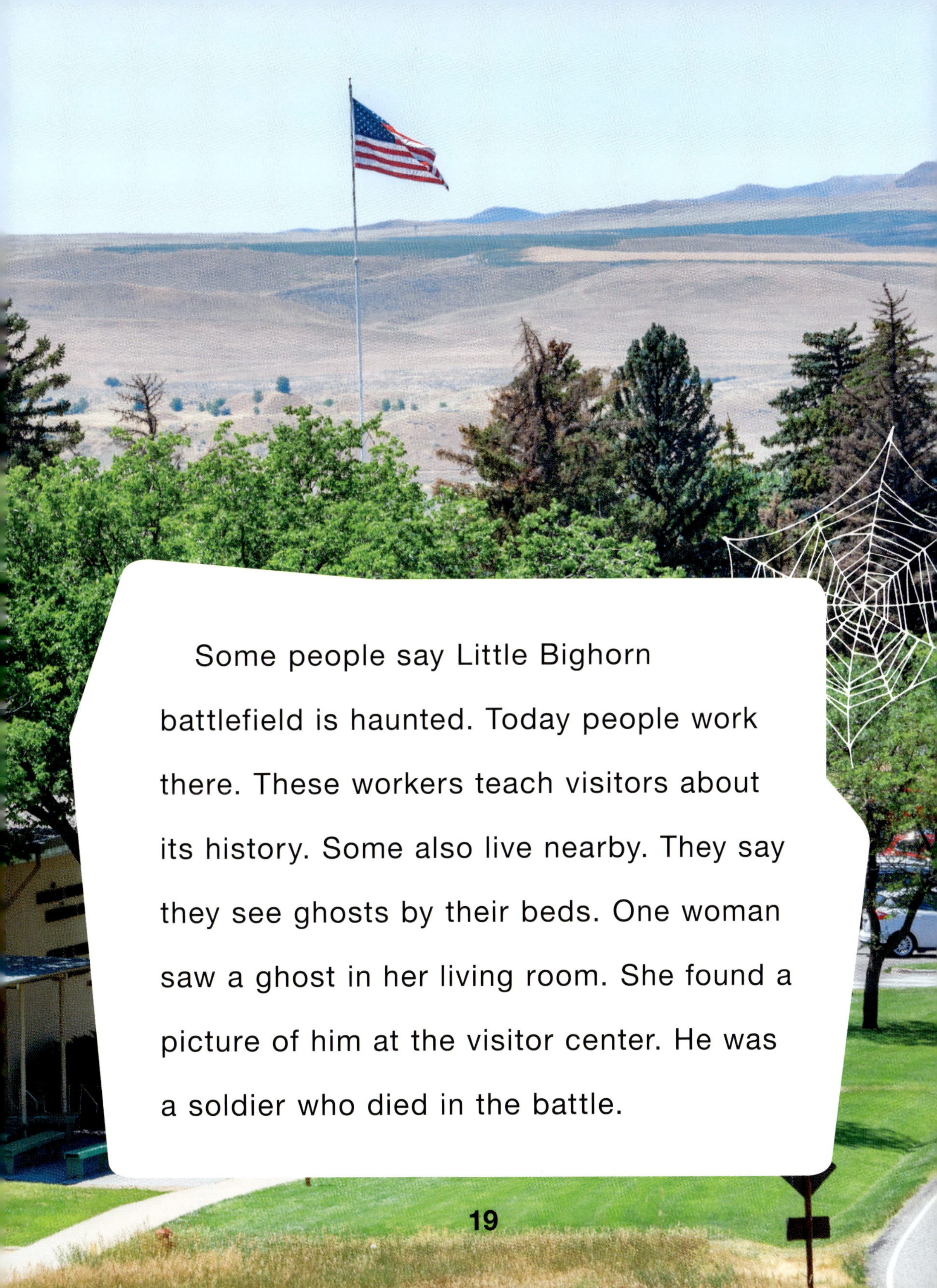

Some people say Little Bighorn battlefield is haunted. Today people work there. These workers teach visitors about its history. Some also live nearby. They say they see ghosts by their beds. One woman saw a ghost in her living room. She found a picture of him at the visitor center. He was a soldier who died in the battle.

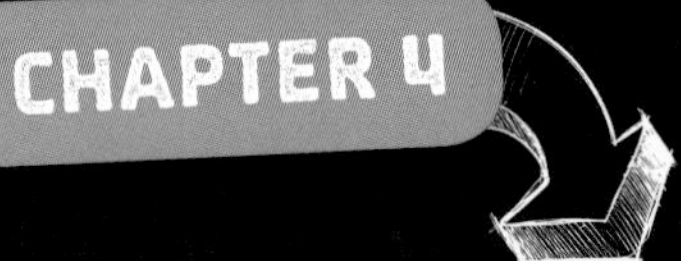

THE GHOSTS OF Cold Harbor

Cold Harbor is in Virginia. A Civil War battle happened there. It took place in 1864. Thousands of soldiers died.

After the battle, people collected the bones of the soldiers who died there.

A LONG FIGHT

The Battle of Cold Harbor lasted 13 days.

Strange events now happen on the battlefield. The sound of horses' hooves can be heard. Cannons boom. The smell of **gunpowder** fills the air.

People travel to visit Cold Harbor. They can tour a nearby house. A family used to live there. Soldiers took over the home. They used it as a hospital. Many soldiers died there. Their bodies are buried in the front lawn. A girl used to live there. She is said to haunt her old home.

CHAPTER 5

THE GHOSTS OF Stalingrad

Stalingrad was a city in Russia. Russia fought Germany in World War II. Germany tried to take the city. They bombed buildings. Almost 2 million people died. Thousands were **civilians**.

There were many fires during the Battle of Stalingrad. Smoke filled the air.

A statue honors the people who died fighting for Stalingrad's freedom.

The Battle of Stalingrad was bloody. It was one of the worst in history. It began in 1942. It lasted almost seven months. Russia won the fight.

Graves from the battle are still being found. People say ghosts haunt the city. The ghosts do not try to scare people. They just go about their business. They act like they are still alive. Some ghosts roam the streets. Others haunt houses that were once their homes.

A NEW NAME

Now the city is called Volgograd.

GLOSSARY

anniversary
the month and day of an event that happened during a previous year

civilian
a person who is not part of the military

grave
a place in the ground where a body is buried

gunpowder
an explosive material used to make guns fire

haunted
having mysterious events happen often, possibly due to visits from ghosts

skeleton
a complete set of bones within the human body

TRIVIA

1. Visitors to Gettysburg can take a train ride across the battlefield. Many riders have seen ghosts near the tracks.
2. People think the land near Culloden is also haunted. A woman who lives there hears soldiers marching at night. She never sees them when she looks out her window.
3. A worker at the Little Bighorn visitor center saw a soldier standing in a corner of the museum. He thought it was another worker playing a joke. But then he saw the soldier walk through a wall!

ACTIVITY

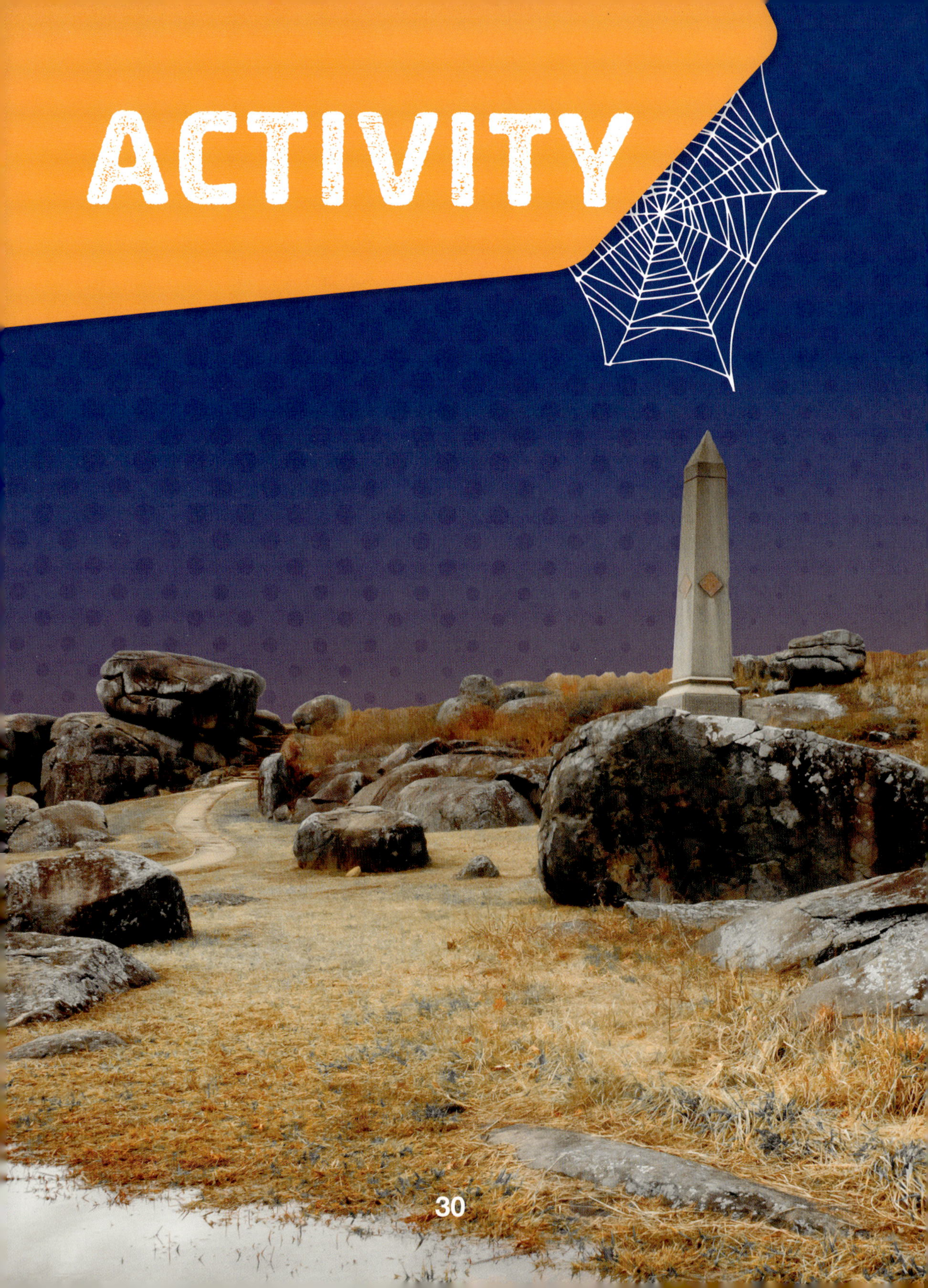

Many people believe some battlefields and other historic places are haunted. Think of a historic place near where you live. If it were haunted, who do you think the ghosts would be? What would they look like? What would they do when they appeared to the living? Write a short story about the ghosts you imagine haunting this historic place. Share your spooky story with a friend!

FURTHER RESOURCES

Want to read more about haunted battlefields? Check out these books:

Ferut, Michael. *Gettysburg*. Minneapolis, Minn.: Bellwether Media, 2014.

Owings, Lisa. *Ghosts in Battlefields*. Minneapolis, Minn.: Bellwether Media, 2017.

Rice, Earle, Jr. *Little Bighorn: History and Legend*. Kennett Square, Penn.: Purple Toad Publishing, 2015.

Think you might want to visit one of the battlefields in this book? Check out these websites:

Culloden, National Trust for Scotland
https://www.nts.org.uk/Visit/Culloden

Gettysburg, National Park Service
https://www.nps.gov/gett/index.htm

Little Bighorn Battlefield, National Park Service
https://www.nps.gov/libi/index.htm

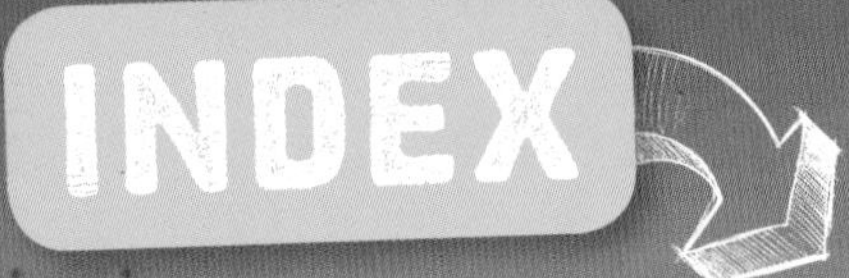